Camille Mobilizes

Jennifer Lagier

FUTURECYCLE PRESS
www.futurecycle.org

Copyright © 2018 Jennifer Lagier
All Rights Reserved

Published by FutureCycle Press
Athens, Georgia, USA

ISBN 978-1-942371-69-4

*"I'm willing to throw my body in front of the bus
to stop bad ideas."*

—*Elizabeth Warren*

Contents

Strange Lonely Men 7
Squatting Over Their Machines 8
Hot Seat 9
Free of That 10
With the Other Old Farts 11
Grass Goes Insane 12
Once You Get the Taste 13
Can't Hear 14
This Tired Machine 15
Our Bodies Were Worn 16
Moving Toward Death 17
Loud Laughing Wenches 18
This Place Has Found Us 19
How Did We Get Here? 20
Better Than Immortality 21
Lean Back Into It 22
No Courage There 23
No Reserves, No Recourse 24
Ponder Our Imbecilities 25
Passion Has Its Own Way 26
The Emperor Has No Clothes 27
Tastes Bitter 28
One Collapses, Surrenders 29
The Unfairness of the Game 30
Forget It 32
Intolerable Conditions 33
Camille's Gratitude List 34
Send it Home 35
The Night the Muse Dumped You 36
Waiting on Death 37

Strange Lonely Men

At the grocery store,
Camille discovers lonesome geezers
forlornly pushing shopping carts,
befuddled by produce.
They're unable to tell the difference
between ripe or green,
melon, peach or tomato.

She wonders if this is how
they once chose their women,
grabbing the showiest specimen
from the top of a pyramid
without consideration
for soundness or sweetness.

How many years before
the magic waned
and they strayed,
substituting a younger version
of the same cardboard model?

Squatting Over Their Machines

Camille can't face
one more Zumba,
circuit training or spin class.
Claims her place among treadmills,
stairmasters, rowing machines.
Opts for sixty minutes on a lifecycle,
goaded by the throbbing beat
of Lady Gaga and Bruno Mars.
Joins red-faced, sweaty compadres.
Most listen to music or read magazines
as they struggle and groan.
Others stare at wall-mounted TVs
where flat screens display
carping presidential candidates,
the latest terrorist attacks,
scrolling ticker tape headlines.
Camille zones out watching "Cupcake Wars."
Pushes her body to burn calories,
trim and tighten problem spots,
delighted by the wicked irony.
Salivates at the construction
of orgasm-inducing,
calorie-laden desserts.

Hot Seat

Camille sits on a squishy sofa
that sends her lower back
into immediate spasm.
Balks at the word "god,"
refuses to recite the serenity prayer
while holding hands with a stranger.

Swallows a lump in her throat
as another woman describes
her alcoholic husband's denial.
Recognizes the sad scenario,
downward spiral.
Decides not to share
her emotions of anger, betrayal.

Agrees with the three Cs:
You didn't create it.
Don't control it.
Can't cure it.

Could kick herself in the ass
for not knowing better.

Free of That

Camille observes twosomes of all ages
meandering the ocean boardwalk,
wonders how they manage to maintain
romantic coupledom over the long run.

She watches white-haired men and women
holding hands, embracing at sunset.
Ponders how they sustain intimacy
from which she feels excluded.

Based on experience, discovers
familiarity steals passion's juices.
Love burns hot and quick,
turns to ash as infatuation weakens.

Knows this is the youngest,
wildest, most playful she'll ever be.
Embraces involuntary independence,
lives it up like a diva.

With the Other Old Farts

Chinaski would be pissed
if he could see how boring
Camille has become.

Lovers arrive infrequently.
Her unused vagina
possibly shriveling up.

The effort of applying makeup,
selecting sexy lingerie
is far too much work.

She's happy wearing second-hand rags,
sharing cheap, early bird dinners
with rude women friends.

Grass Goes Insane

An armed security guard
at the medical marijuana dispensary
looks Camille over, checks her ID.
He reiterates their cash-only policy,
allows customers into the showroom,
two at a time.

Apothecary jars display
potent buds of dried weed,
imaginative edibles, extracts,
grass in its many incarnations:
sativa, indica, ruderalis.

The shelves are stocked
with assorted oils,
vape cartridges,
pre-rolled joints,
jars of pure THC.

A special nook features
tinctures to ease pain, stimulate appetite,
erase anxiety, treat insomnia.
Others address epilepsy, nausea, PTSD.

Camille chooses from a smorgasbord
of dope delicacies, looks forward
to a weekend sampling
her cannabis treasure trove,
all the ways to get high.

Once You Get the Taste

Camille is sick
of hearing excuses.
Is fed up with pharmacists
who won't answer their phone
or communicate with her doctor.
Can't bear the thought
of one more blood test,
mammogram, X-ray.
Is convinced pinot noir
is a better mood stabilizer
than Zoloft, Lexapro, Prozac.
Has decided to stop
holding her tongue,
being polite,
putting up with alarmist
endocrinologist bullshit.
Rejects civility
when confronted
with condescending physicians.
Doesn't care
if she is rude,
disruptive,
hurts some incompetent
phlebotomist's feelings.
Swears off traditional medicine.
Turns to exercise, natural remedies.
Avoids laboratories, specialists,
outpatient clinics.

Can't Hear

Camille complains about
her mumbling lover.
Swears the TV is turned too low.
Is frustrated when friends reveal
juicy secrets she can't decipher,
blames noisy restaurants.

Irritated, she submits
to an audiologist's testing.
Is pissed to discover
a profound hearing loss
that can't be explained.

On the bright side,
she considers Fox News blaring
from every gym monitor,
offensive asides in the weight room,
the benefits of deafness when surrounded
by loud, low-IQ men.

This Tired Machine

Camille swears the aging laptop,
sporadically functional Fitbit,
have declared a fatwa against her.
They sabotage writing and exercise,
life-saving mental health outlets.

At night, garden twinkle lights
commit suicide by power surge,
flameless candles devour D batteries,
leave her with unreliable illumination
or in total darkness.

Her tired body betrays:
osteoporotic hips ache,
finger joints freeze,
cervix and vagina shrivel
like dehydrated flowers.

"Ah, my golden years!" she intones,
imbibes liquid THC
with a chaser of Tylenol,
two Melatonin,
Lexapro nightcap.

Our Bodies Were Worn

Daily, Camille sees Brody
limping into the gym.
He totters unevenly
from station to station
pumps iron with
his weak arm and leg,
slowly regains strength
after having a stroke.

They nod in passing,
grunt during workouts,
grimace and make noises
that remind her of sex.

His blue eyes follow her progress
at resistance training machines.
She performs flies, curls, crunches.
He stares at her erect nipples.
Despite tight jogging bra,
they make themselves known.

She imagines him naked,
involuntarily moistens.
Visualizes him between her thighs.
Wonders if endorphin overload
and celibacy overdose
have damaged her brain.

Moving Toward Death

Camille recognizes the slow dance
toward undignified mortality.
Despises drooping breasts,
multiplying wrinkles,
slight incontinence
when she laughs or sneezes.

Laments thinning hair,
proliferation of age spots.
Wonders how long
before sex drive evaporates,
mobility shrinks,
short-term memory vanishes.

Refuses to relinquish
sardonic personality,
caustic opinions,
hard-won independence.

Seeks disillusioned rebels
with an affinity for
weed, wine and irreverence
to join her crone revolution.

Loud Laughing Wenches

Camille wallows in sangria,
cynicism and Amy Winehouse.
Until tonight, didn't realize
she'd exceeded her expiry date.
Regrets unconsummated lust
she has squandered.
Contemplates a sexless tomorrow.

Young wenches at Doc Ricketts'
crowd the bar, cadge free drinks
from horny tourists out slumming.
Display their long legs,
hot-pink toenails,
uplifted cleavage.

Camille remembers taut, carefree youth,
turning heads, fending off passes.
Surveys the sorry lot of sodden men
spilling beer and complaining.
Sighs, buys her own glass of wine.
Will take herself home for a night
of old schmaltzy movies.

This Place Has Found Us

Camille watches The Donald
cozying up to Sarah Palin,
Tea Party darling,
maverick moron.

It's amazing that much stupid
in a confined space
doesn't implode the skulls
of cheering fans
who gather around them.

Camille wishes she had a toke
to erase coming months
of campaign chatter,
political pandering.

Regrets going dry
at a time when
she desperately needs
a prolonged bender,
then sustained blackout.

How Did We Get Here?

Camille listens to
potential commanders-in-chief
defile her television screen,
quibble over the size
of the front-runner's penis.
Argue how rapidly
they would deploy troops,
deny abortion,
deport immigrant workers.
Advocate banning Muslims,
killing off health care.
Boast about embracing
more enhanced torture.
Pledge to target
terrorists' families
for state-sanctioned murder.
Describe vague solutions
to manufactured non-problems.
Pander to bigots.
Reach out to haters.
Brag, ramble and gloat.
Revel in each other's stumbles.
Offer the electorate,
invisible women,
a rickety clown car
of terrible choices.

Better Than Immortality

> "Just when you think Donald Trump's opinions about women and their rights had reached rock bottom, he managed to quarry even further into some ring of hell that, until previously, only existed in Dante's *Inferno*."
> —Stassa Edwards, *The Slot*

The Donald declares
he is pro-life,
pronounces abortions
should be banned and
women who have them
must be shamed,
individually *punished*.

It's time for the righteous
to return knocked-up broads
to those *back-alley places*
where they used to go
before a bunch of liberal judges
with no respect for the unborn
gave these sluts a choice,
allowed them to terminate
the fruit of their sins.

He doesn't believe in exceptions
for rape or incest.
Let them reap what they sow.
No consequences for men;
it's not their issue.

Camille grits her teeth,
donates to Planned Parenthood,
sends Elizabeth Warren
a huge contribution.

Lean Back Into It

> *Are Trump Supporters Too Dumb to Know They're Dumb? Science Says 'Probably'* —headline from *Addicting Info* article

Camille vapes Sunset Tea marijuana,
watches presidential candidates debate.
She hits the mute button,
improvises moronic non-sequiturs
in the voice of Daffy Duck
on behalf of The Donald.
Invents a pornographic response.

Sick of lies,
mischaracterizations,
political pandering,
she wants to erase
the indelible image
of Trump's white supremacist,
illiterate, misogynistic supporters
as they strut and preen,
spew virulent hatred
on prime-time TV.

She's had her fill of
impotent moderators,
spin-doctor pundits,
middle-school squabbles
with lethal implications
for a healthy planet,
any person of conscience.

No Courage There

Camille savors the vision
of prominent Republicans
contradicting The Donald
when confronted
by news anchors
on network TV.

Politicians attempt to backpedal
the would-be Groper in Chief
as he vehemently insists
the election is rigged,
denies brutish behavior
captured on video,
calls women nasty, fat pigs.

One by one, die-hard supporters
piously voice disapproval
of sexual harassment, assault.
They hide behind "decency"
but refuse to pull their endorsements.

No Reserves, No Recourse

Camille cannot bear to hear
one more vicious gaffe
from The Donald
and his raving supporters.

Feels her final vestige
of tolerance implode
as an electoral train wreck
careens off the tracks.

To prevent total breakdown,
disconnects from the grid.
Boycotts papers, political blogs,
non-stop TV news.

Replaces sensational headlines with
a banana smoothie vaporizer,
streaming classic movies,
Good Vibrations sex toy.

In her time-warp cocoon,
Camille shuts out the world,
trades annoyance for ignorant bliss,
savors nourishing calm.

Ponder Our Imbecilities

Camille is depressed, disillusioned.
Rations news consumption to less
than fifteen minutes a day.
Cannot bear to hear one more
idiotic conspiracy theory.

Has no patience with
screaming shock jocks
inciting violent hate crimes
against lesbians, transgendered, gays,
women, liberals, people of color.

If she has to watch another
bloated white man over 60
smirk, lie through his teeth,
she'll fling something heavy
through her TV.

Passion Has Its Own Way

Camille has vowed
to give wide berth
to the terminally stupid.
Finds herself unable
to bite her tongue,
listen politely to one more
opinionated moron lacking experience,
knowledge or facts.

She grits her teeth
overhearing remarks
spewed by the arrogantly clueless.
Especially those whose decisions
negatively impact her safety,
sanity, self-respect,
financial resources.

Camille loses sleep
as women's rights
are continuously
overturned or eroded.
Vows to seek out
equally infuriated sisters,
focus what energy
she has left to organize, mobilize,
shut down the machine.

The Emperor Has No Clothes

Putin's puppet demands adulation,
military hardware as inauguration accessories,
redecorates the White House
to include golden curtains.

In this post-factual era,
fake news reigns,
black becomes white,
deception the norm,
science and statistics supplanted
by self-serving fictions.

He insists we live in terror,
accept incremental repression,
normalize dismantlement of democracy,
approve attacks on political scapegoats.

Camille and millions of women around the world disagree,
demonstrate, refuse to recognize
an illegitimately installed groper-in-chief,
his exaggerations and falsehoods.

Resistance breaks the spell,
reveals naked truth:
the emperor has no clothes;
there is power in numbers.

Tastes Bitter

The newly-anointed Cheeto-in-chief
surrounds himself with authoritarian white men,
signs draconian orders—
issues a global gag rule,
complete rollback of environmental protections,
disconnects the public comments switchboard,
scrubs White House website.

On Day Two,
he claims millions voted illegally,
short-lists potential Supreme Court justices,
rabid conservatives favoring curtailment
of First Amendment rights, civil liberties,
unreasonable searches and seizures.
He green-lights controversial pipelines,
bans federal agencies from social media,
insists on a total news blackout.

California's Governor calls out
Trump's universe of non-facts.
Constitutional experts document
President Pussy Grabber's violation
of the emoluments clause, file a lawsuit.

Camille vows not to take these assaults lying down.
Bombards legislators with volatile phone calls.

One Collapses, Surrenders

It's another gray day:
potential nuclear war with North Korea,
more lethal grammar school shootouts,
demagogues relaxing regulations,
poisoning food, air and water.

Headlines blare fresh atrocities:
barrel bombs, drone-delivered assassinations,
saber rattling white men
thumbing their noses at psychotic dictators,
backdoor attacks on healthcare,
abortion, civil liberties.

Ivanka and Jared,
Barbie and Ken dolls with political clout,
research personalities, trends
on clickbait news sites, Amazon, Google,
play diplomat, statesman,
walk away with profitable contracts,
trademark agreements.

President Pussy Grabber
demotes white supremacist
and scary skank,
blusters and tweets.
Spicey spins alt reality as poll numbers
drop into free fall.

Camille persists, resists,
does her best to pull the rug
out from underneath a shit show
featuring Putin's puppet
and his amateur cast
of corrupt pretenders.

The Unfairness of the Game

> "There's a group of guys in a back room somewhere that are making decisions." —Sen. Claire McCaskill

Thirteen Republican white men
hide behind a locked door as they
craft a bill to control women's bodies.

They operate in a vacuum of facts,
base legislation on lethal ignorance,
disproved urban legends:

*If it's a legitimate rape, the female body
has ways to try to shut that whole thing down.*

*Who needs abortion when victims of sexual assault
can just get "cleaned out" by a rape kit?*

*Women shouldn't terminate pregnancies
resulting from rape because it's what God intended.*

*Abortion is much more serious
than the rape of children by priests.*

Abortion rights caused the Sandy Hook massacre.

Abortion is just like the Holocaust.

If babies had guns, they wouldn't be aborted.

*Rape is okay when the victim seems
"older than her chronological age."*

*Getting an abortion after being raped
is criminal evidence tampering.*

Senators refuse to share a draft
for review or public comment.
"We aren't stupid," says a GOP aide.

Camille and women with prior experience,
so much to lose, have a different opinion.

Forget It

Camille fumes while Pussy-Grabber-in-Chief
floods cyberspace
with insane Tourette tweets.
Spineless legislators help
deconstruct federal government,
pander to neo-Nazis, conspiracy nuts.

Critical thinking and civility
succumb within the gas chambers
of faux Fox News
under leadership
of smug white male harassers
bankrolled by rich bottom-feeders.

Forget an era of tolerance,
diversity, social justice.
Rabid reactionaries have
staged a successful coup.
The American Dream
is officially over.

Intolerable Conditions

> "The right thing to do is pray in moments like this."
> —Paul Ryan

Camille reads moronic responses
to the latest assault weapon slaughter,
implores the goddess
to intercede, impose sanity,
vaporize clueless males.

She is fed up with
Second Amendment fanatics
who fail to comprehend that automatic guns
capable of mowing down hundreds
had not been invented
when the Constitution was written.

Camille fantasizes a sea of white
Republican men on their knees,
begging to be spared as she smiles,
presses the trigger of her AK-47,
targets hypocrisy, drops them like flies.

Camille's Gratitude List

She gives thanks
for free-spirited,
mature, lusty men.

Takes joy in
a functioning pleasure zone,
testament to effective,
if expensive, estrogen cream.

Compliments her own
tiny nipples,
still-perky breasts.

Praises power walks
along the Pacific
that keep her ass
toned and undimpled.

Counts herself fortunate
to still possess
a supple mind,
wry sense of humor,
all her organs and teeth.

Send it Home

Camille has power walked
through jungle coconut palms,
spooked a flurry of egrets
who now twist their beady eyes,
watch her sweaty, uphill progress
from where they perch
on plumeria branches.

Earlier, she made love
as trade winds blew in
through an open door,
platinum lightning splintered
darkness over calm ocean.

Now she sips hot coffee,
pounds the keyboard
of her computer.
Transfers photos
to friends back home.
Immigrates to a saner land.
Evades drab dystopia.

The Night the Muse Dumped You

Camille has nothing,
imagination's needle on empty.
She reads, revises, discards.
Pounds flaccid keyboard.
Prays for a miracle.

She has exceeded her
creative shelf life.
Now it's nothing but rejects
from English majors
enrolled in Literary Magazine 2
to fluff their own vitae.

"Didn't I warn you?"
sneers a sadistic inner Nazi
who taunts by revealing
the virginal page
she will never deflower.

Her dominatrix muse
bends Camille over the desk,
uncoils a dark whip,
flourishes red-ink editorial pen,
makes her aching soul suffer.

Waiting on Death

Camille has no intention
of going out with a whimper.
She'll burn her candle
at both ends,
create maximum uproar.

She imagines gleefully
working her way
down a bucket list
of rude, crude and lewd,
breaking rules with abandon.

Signs up for a nudist weekend,
erotic belly dancing lessons,
an afternoon of sky diving,
restyles her hair to include
lavender highlights.

She sips signature pinot noir
at her favorite bistro, trolls
for an adventuresome playmate
who appreciates, shares
her outrageous intentions.

Acknowledgments

The author is grateful to the following publishers where some of this work originally appeared, sometimes in a slightly different version.

ARTMAG: "Free of That"
Dead Snakes: "Moving Toward Death," "This Place Has Found Us," "Better Than Immortality"
I Am Not a Silent Poet: "Tastes Bitter"
In Between Hangovers: "Strange Lonely Men," "Once You Get the Taste," "Our Bodies Were Worn," "Lean Back Into It," "No Courage There," "The Night the Muse Dumped You," "Ponder Our Imbecilities," "Passion Has Its Own Way," "Waiting on Death"
Rat's Ass Review: "The Emperor Has No Clothes"
Rockford Review: "No Reserves, No Recourse"
Winedrunk Sidewalk: "One Collapses, Surrenders," "The Unfairness of the Game," "Forget It"
Your One Phone Call: "Loud Laughing Wenches," "How Did We Get Here?"

Cover artwork by Gene McCormick; cover and interior book design by Diane Kistner; Calisto MT text and Belotta titling

About FutureCycle Press

FutureCycle Press is dedicated to publishing lasting English-language poetry books, chapbooks, and anthologies in both print-on-demand and Kindle ebook formats. Founded in 2007 by long-time independent editor/publishers and partners Diane Kistner and Robert S. King, the press incorporated as a nonprofit in 2012. A number of our editors are distinguished poets and writers in their own right, and we have been actively involved in the small press movement going back to the early seventies.

The FutureCycle Poetry Book Prize and honorarium is awarded annually for the best full-length volume of poetry we publish in a calendar year. Introduced in 2013, our Good Works projects are anthologies devoted to issues of universal significance, with all proceeds donated to a related worthy cause. Our Selected Poems series highlights contemporary poets with a substantial body of work to their credit; with this series we strive to resurrect work that has had limited distribution and is now out of print.

We are dedicated to giving all of the authors we publish the care their work deserves, making our catalog of titles the most diverse and distinguished it can be, and paying forward any earnings to fund more great books.

We've learned a few things about independent publishing over the years. We've also evolved a unique, resilient publishing model that allows us to focus mainly on vetting and preserving for posterity poetry collections of exceptional quality without becoming overwhelmed with bookkeeping and mailing, fundraising activities, or taxing editorial and production "bubbles." To find out more about what we are doing, come see us at www.futurecycle.org.